Texas Style Recipes

A Complete Cookbook of Southwest
Dish Ideas!

Table of Contents

The desserts are somehow tastier in Texas than they seem to be everywhere else... Here are some of the best...

Introduction

Do you think you'd like to bring the taste of Texas to your own home, wherever that may be?

Can you successfully replicate the cooking methods, ingredients and style of Texas dishes?

You certainly can! Starting with breakfast, you'll find that croissants and coffee are not standard fare here. Breakfasts include things like French toast, biscuits with butter and jam, and dishes that include typical ingredients like eggs, bacon and potatoes.

In the Lone Star State, the largest meal of their day is often dinner, which is served mid-day. The menu may include dishes with BBQ spare ribs or fried chicken, fried okra, corn bread and sliced tomatoes… and Texas desserts are SO tasty, including homemade ice cream and pecan pie.

Why is Texas food so good?

It's because the people in Texas genuinely enjoy eating. Since they like to eat, they will not settle for anything less than foods that are pleasing to them.

Beans are used quite often in Texas cooking. Pinto beans are used commonly, whether they are refried, mashed, baked or boiled. They are often served with corn bread. They can appear in any meal, but beans are especially valuable to Tex-Mex and barbeque meals.

There is so much more to Texas cooking than can be covered in one cookbook, but I've tried to include some of the best recipes, and those true to the state. Sample them soon!

Texans love their breakfast, and they have many different recipes for morning meals... Try a couple of these...

1 – Texas Breakfast Tacos

These tacos are not built to be aesthetically pleasing – they include many foods in a small foil wrapping. Soft tortillas are stuffed with many types of goodies, and then closed to keep them warm and keep those goodies from falling out while you eat.

Makes 6 Servings

Cooking + Prep Time: 40 minutes

Ingredients:

- 6 tortillas, flour
- 1/2-lb. of ground breakfast sausage
- 6 scrambled eggs, large
- 6 bacon slices
- 1 medium potato, cubed, with skin left on
- 1/4 tsp. of salt, kosher
- 1/8 tsp. of cumin
- 1/4 tsp. of garlic powder
- 1/2 tsp. of onion powder
- 3/4 tsp. of chili powder
- 12 tbsp. of Colby Jack cheese shreds

Instructions:

1. Mix potato seasonings. Set them aside.

2. Scramble the eggs. Brown sausage.

3. After cooking, transfer sausage and eggs to covered dishes so they'll stay moist and warm.

4. Discard all but 2 tbsp. of fat from sausage pan. Add cubed potatoes to that fat in the pan you used for sausage.

5. Toss and coat. Sprinkle on the seasoning blend and stir frequently till each side of potato cubes is covered.

6. Cook potatoes in lidded pan on med. heat till potatoes are tender and browned, or about 12-15 minutes. Stir them frequently so they won't burn.

7. After cooking, remove lid from potatoes. Allow them to rest on lowest setting.

8. Warm the flour tortillas in hot pan.

9. Store tortillas in warmer or simply cover, to retain moisture and heat.

10. Unroll six foil pieces, a bit larger than your tortillas.

11. Place one warm flour tortilla in middle of each foil piece.

12. Add 1/6 each ingredient in center of tortillas.

13. Fold tortillas over and close them. Snugly roll foil around taco, forming closed cylinder and keep in a warmed oven till serving.

2 – Texas French Toast

This is a classic Texas breakfast, and it's as tasty as it is easy. It **Makes** a wonderful weekend morning meal, and a sweet treat for brunch, as well.

Makes 4 Servings

Cooking + Prep Time: 25 minutes

Ingredients:

- 1 cup of milk, whole
- 4 eggs, large

- 2 tsp. of vanilla, pure
- 2 tbsp. of sugar, granulated
- 1/2 tsp. of cinnamon, ground
- 1/2 tsp. of orange zest
- 1/4 tsp. of nutmeg, ground
- 8 slices of Texas toast
- 2 tbsp. of butter, unsalted
- Syrup, maple flavored

Instructions:

1. Whisk first seven ingredients together in shallow bowl. Dip the slices of bread into the egg mixture and turn to coat. Allow each slice to soak in the egg mixture for 10 sec. each side.

2. Melt 1 tbsp. butter in skillet on med. heat. Add 1/2 of bread slices and cook for two to three minutes per side, till golden brown. Remove bread from skillet.

3. Repeat using the rest of the butter and slices of bread. Serve warm with syrup.

3 – Southwest Breakfast Casserole

This recipe is quite easy, especially if you prepare it the previous night and then just bake it the next morning. Unlike many egg casseroles, this one is not at all dry – it's deliciously moist.

Makes 8 Servings

Cooking + Prep Time: 1 hour & 5 minutes

Ingredients:

- 1 x 7-ounce can of mild chilies
- 1 x 4-ounce can of mild chilies
- 8 strip-cut tortillas, corn

- 1 x 12-ounce pkg. of cooked, drained breakfast sausage
- 1 diced, medium onion, yellow
- 8 eggs, large
- 1/2 cup of whipping cream, heavy
- 1 tsp. of cumin, ground
- 1/2 tsp. of black pepper, ground
- 1/2 tsp. of salt, kosher
- 1/2 tsp. of garlic powder
- 1 & 1/2 cups of pepper jack blend cheese shreds
- 2 sliced, small Roma tomatoes
- 1/2 tsp. of paprika, sweet

Optional:

- Pico de Gallo sauce
- Sour cream

Instructions:

1. Coat 13" x 9" baking dish lightly using non-stick cooking spray. Layer a half of chilies, then tortilla strips, then sausage and onion, and cheese last, in baking dish.

2. Repeat layering a second time, using up remainder of ingredients in step 1.

3. Whisk the cream, eggs, kosher salt, ground pepper, cumin and garlic salt together till combined well. Pour the mixture over the casserole.

4. Arrange the sliced tomatoes on the top. Sprinkle over them with the paprika. Cover with cling wrap. Refrigerate overnight.

5. Next day, heat the oven to 350F. Remove the cling wrap. Bake the casserole for 35-40 minutes till center sets and edges brown lightly.

6. Serve with Pico de Gallo and/or sour cream, if desired.

4 – Oat & Raspberry Breakfast Bars

For another sweet breakfast option, here are fruit topped Texas breakfast bars. The raspberry topping is tart, but you can add sugar to your topping if you like or use blueberries or blackberries for their sweetness.

Makes 12 Servings

Cooking + Prep Time: 50 minutes

Ingredients:

- 1/2 cup of lightly toasted coconut, shredded
- 1 & 1/2 cups of flour, whole wheat
- 1 cup of oats, old-fashioned
- 1/4 tsp. of salt, kosher
- 1/2 cup of sugar, brown
- 1 egg, large
- 1/2 cup of melted butter, unsalted
- 2 tbsp. of milk, 2%
- 6 oz. of raspberries, fresh or frozen

Instructions:

1. Preheat the oven up to 350 degrees F. Then line one 9" square baking pan using foil. Spray using non-stick spray.

2. Toast the coconut on the foil at 350F for three to five minutes. Remove pan from the oven. Set it aside.

3. Combine flour, coconut, oats, granulated sugar and kosher salt in bowl. Combine egg, milk & butter in small sized bowl. Stir wet ingredients in with dry ingredients till you have formed a dough.

4. Reserve 3/4 cup of dough. Press the rest into the pan evenly.

5. Mash the raspberries in small sized bowl. Spread over the dough in the pan. Crumble reserved dough on top of raspberry layer.

6. Bake for 25 to 30 minutes, till the bars turn a golden brown. Allow to cool, then cut and serve.

5 – Texas Breakfast Hash

This hash is served often at breakfast time but can also be a suitable dish for brunch. If you would like yours to be smoky, you can add a couple chipotle peppers. That'll certainly wake everyone up!

Makes 4 Servings

Cooking + Prep Time: 35 minutes

Ingredients:

- 4 peeled and diced potatoes
- 1/2-pound of sausage, breakfast

- 8 thick-cut bacon slices, diced
- 3 diced garlic cloves
- 1 diced onion, white
- 2 sliced jalapeños, fresh
- 2 minced chipotle peppers
- 1/2 sliced bunch of green onions
- 1 tsp. of seasoning, creole
- 1 tsp. of onion powder
- 1 tsp. of garlic powder
- 1/2 tsp. of chili powder
- 1/2 tsp. of pepper, ground
- 1/4 tsp. of red pepper, crushed
- 1 cup of grated cheddar cheese

Instructions:

1. Add the diced potatoes to med. pot. Cover them with cool water. Boil them for five minutes, then drain them and set them aside.

2. Add 1 tbsp. oil to med. skillet. Heat on med. Add the bacon. Cook till it is crispy. Drain the bacon. Set it aside.

3. Reserve only 2 tbsp. of the bacon grease. Add jalapeños, onions and chipotle peppers. Sauté them for five minutes and add garlic. Sauté for a minute more.

4. Add the breakfast sausage. Cook till browned. Add the potatoes and all the spices.

5. Combine the mixture well. Cook for five minutes or so and stir it occasionally.

6. Heat the broiler. Add bacon and 1/2 green onions into the potato mixture. Add cheese on top. Place mixture under the broiler for three to four minutes, till the cheese has melted. Remove from the oven. Sprinkle with the remainder of green onions. Add sour cream and serve.

Sometimes the meals are bigger in Texas, too. Here are some of their best lunch, dinner, side dish and appetizer recipes...

6 – Tex-Mex Dip

It's hard to beat Texas classic seven-layer dip when you're in the mood for a protein-filled snack. It's been a favorite for a very long time and is still quite popular today.

Makes 7 Servings

Cooking + Prep Time: 1/2 hour or less

Ingredients:

- 1 x 16-oz. can of beans, refried
- 1 cup of guacamole

- 1/4 cup of mayonnaise, reduced fat
- 1 x 8-oz. container of sour cream, low sodium
- 1 packet of seasoning mix, taco flavor
- 2 cups of cheddar cheese shreds
- 1 chopped tomato
- 1/4 cup of chopped onions, green
- 1/4 cup of drained olives, black

Instructions:

1. Spread beans in large sized serving dish. Layer guacamole over the top.

2. Mix sour cream, mayonnaise and seasoning mix in medium sized bowl. Spread this over top of guacamole.

3. Sprinkle one layer of cheese shreds over sour cream mix layer. Sprinkle over top of cheese with tomatoes, green onion & olives. Serve.

7 – Texas Chili

This is a spicy, classic chili in the style of Texas. It does not contain ground beef, beans or tomatoes, but it still tastes great on cold days. If you prefer your chili without beer, you can use water in the same amount, if you like.

Makes 8 Servings

Cooking + Prep Time: 3 & 1/2 hours

Ingredients:

- 4 chopped bacon slices
- 2 chopped onions
- 8 chopped garlic cloves
- 2 tsp. of oregano, dried
- 1 tsp. of pepper, cayenne
- 3 tbsp. of paprika, hot
- 1/3 cup of chili powder
- 1 tbsp. of cumin, ground
- 4 lbs. of cubed beef chuck roast, boneless
- 4 & 3/4 cups of water, filtered
- 1 x 12-oz. can of beer, your choice of brand
- 4 canned, de-seeded, minced Chipotle peppers with adobo sauce
- 2 tbsp. of corn meal

Instructions:

1. Cook the bacon on med. heat in heavy pot till it is crispy. Drain off any excess grease but leave sufficient amount to cover bottom of pan.

2. Add garlic and onions. Stir while cooking till onions become tender. Season them with cumin, chili powder,

paprika, cayenne pepper and oregano. Stir while cooking for 35 seconds till the spices are toasted.

3. Add and stir water, beef, peppers, beer (or extra water) and corn meal and bring to boil. Lower heat down to low. Leave uncovered and simmer for 2 & 1/2 – 3 hours, till the beef becomes tender. Serve hot.

8 – Armadillo Eggs

These aren't real armadillo eggs, of course. They are jalapeño peppers, stuffed with so many goodies that you don't know where to start when you sit down to eat.

Makes 8 Servings

Cooking + Prep Time: 1 & 1/4 hour

Ingredients:

- 1/4 cup of bacon bits
- 1 x 8-oz. pkg. of softened cream cheese
- 1 tsp. of hot sauce
- 1 tbsp. of chopped chives, fresh
- 1 lb. of sausage, pork
- 1 cup of cheddar cheese shreds
- 1 x 5 & 1/2-oz. pkg. of coating mix, seasoned
- 1/8 tsp. of cumin, ground
- 1/8 tsp. of chili powder
- 15 jalapeño peppers, fresh

Instructions:

1. Preheat the oven to 350F.

2. Mix cream cheese, chives, hot sauce and bacon bits in medium bowl.

3. In separate bowl, mix cheese and uncooked sausage.

4. On flat work surface, mix chili powder, cumin and coating mix.

5. Cut lengthways slits in peppers. Remove seeds. Stuff peppers with cream cheese and bacon bit mixture. Press sausage mixture around stuffed jalapeño peppers. Roll in coating mix and coat well.

6. Arrange coated jalapeños on cookie sheet in one layer. Bake in 350F oven for 25 minutes till sausage has browned evenly. Serve.

9 – Texas Chicken Chilaquiles

This recipe uses rotisserie chicken from the local grocery to create an easier recipe. The dish is considered to be a comfort food in Texas. It's made with not just chicken, but also tasty salsa, along with tortilla chips, cilantro, jalapeños and tomatillos.

Makes 6-8 Servings

Cooking + Prep Time: 50 minutes

Ingredients:

- 1 lb. of peeled, quartered tomatillos
- 1 peeled, chopped onion, yellow
- 1 jalapeño pepper
- 4 peeled garlic cloves
- 3 tbsp. of oil, olive
- Salt, kosher
- 1 cilantro bunch – discard stems
- 1 tbsp. of cumin, ground
- 1 tbsp. of Mexican oregano, dried
- As needed: chicken broth
- 1 skinned, de-boned rotisserie chicken, whole
- 1 x 9-oz. bag of tortilla chips
- 1 cup of feta cheese crumbles

To serve:

- Crema (Mexican sour cream)
- Pico de Gallo

Instructions:

1. Heat oven to 425F.

2. Combine tomatillos, jalapeño, onion and garlic in large sized, oven-safe skillet. Toss with oil & use salt to season as desired. Roast till tomatillos have browned and have lost most juices, usually 15-20 minutes.

3. Add and stir oregano, cilantro and cumin. Discard jalapeño stems. If skillet seems too dry, add the chicken broth, a bit at a time, and moisten.

4. Add cilantro. Use immersion blender to puree till mixture has the consistency of chunky salsa. You can add more broth here, too, if you need it.

5. Add chips and chicken. Stir till chips are coated completely with the sauce and break into thick paste consistency.

6. Top mixture with the feta cheese. Return pan to oven till cheese has lightly browned and is starting to melt. Serve with Pico de Gallo and crema.

10 – Texas Cole Slaw

This is a favorite with Texans, and you may love it, too. It's a wonderful side dish for picnics and barbeques. If you prefer a milder taste, you can cut back on the number of green onions you use.

Makes 8 Servings

Cooking + Prep Time: 1 hour & 20 minutes

Ingredients:

- 1 cup of mayonnaise, light
- 1 tbsp. of lime juice, fresh

- 1 tbsp. of cumin, ground
- 1 tsp. of salt, kosher
- 1 tsp. of pepper, cayenne
- 1 tsp. of pepper, ground
- 1 rinsed, sliced medium cabbage head
- 1 large shredded carrot
- 2 sliced green onions
- 2 sliced radishes

Instructions:

1. Whisk mayo, lime juice, cumin, kosher salt & both types of pepper in large sized bowl.

2. Add cabbage, green onions, carrot & radishes. Stir till combined well. Chill for an hour or more before you serve.

11 – Texas Guacamole

The perfectly ripe avocados make this a guacamole you'll look forward to making for your family and friends. It also includes red onions, chilies, cilantro and lime juice. It goes well with Tex-Mex and tortilla chip recipes.

Makes 6 Servings

Cooking + Prep Time: 20 minutes

Ingredients:

- 3 halved, pitted avocados, ripe
- 1/4 diced large onion, red

- 2 chopped cloves of garlic
- 2 juiced limes, fresh
- 1 seeded, diced habanero pepper
- 3 tbsp. of cilantro, chopped
- Kosher salt & ground pepper, as desired

Instructions:

1. Place the avocadoes in medium-sized bowl. Mash till they're the consistency you prefer, smooth or chunky.

2. Add and stir lime juice, garlic, onions, cilantro and habanero. Season as desired and serve with tortilla chips.

12 – Jalapeño Sausage Poppers

Once your family and guests get a taste of these poppers, you'll probably be asked to bring them to every get-together. Using toothpicks **Makes** the bacon-wrapped, stuffed jalapeños more secure and easier to eat.

Makes 20 Servings

Cooking + Prep Time: 1 & 1/2 hours

Ingredients:

- 2 x 12-oz. pkgs. of sausage, ground
- 2 x 8-oz. pkgs. of softened cream cheese, light
- 30 jalapeño peppers

- 1 lb. of halved bacon slices

Instructions:

1. Preheat the oven to 375F.

2. Place sausage in large skillet. Cook on med-high till browned evenly.

3. Drain the sausage. Place it in medium-sized bowl and mix with cream cheese.

4. Halve jalapeños lengthways and remove their seeds. Stuff halves with sausage & cream cheese mixture.

5. Wrap the stuffed jalapeños with halved bacon slices and secure them using toothpicks.

6. Arrange the wrapped jalapeños in large baking dish. Bake in 375F oven for 18 to 20 minutes, till bacon has browned evenly. Serve.

13 – Texas Creamed Corn

This is a favorite side with barbeques in the summer, when corn is very much in season. In the colder months of fall and winter, it is served often as a comfort food.

Makes 8 Servings

Cooking + Prep Time: 15 minutes

Ingredients:

- 8 oz. of cubed cream cheese
- 1/2 cup of cubed butter, unsalted
- 1 cup of milk, whole

- 1 tbsp. of sugar, granulated
- 1/2 tsp. of pepper, cayenne
- Salt, kosher & pepper, ground, as desired
- 6 cups of sweet corn, fresh, canned or frozen

Instructions:

1. Melt the butter with cream cheese in pan on med-high.

2. Reduce the heat down to med. Add and stir milk, cayenne pepper and sugar. Season as desired. Add the corn. Stir for about five minutes and serve.

14 – BBQ Brisket

This recipe comes from West Texas, and the meat is delicious and tender. If you happen to have leftovers (don't count on that), the seasoned meat **Makes** super sandwiches.

Makes 8-10 Servings

Cooking + Prep Time: 6 hours & 15 minutes + 8 hours marinating time

Ingredients:

- 2 tbsp. of flavoring, liquid smoke
- 4 lbs. of beef brisket, lean
- 1 tbsp. of salt, onion
- 1 tbsp. of salt, garlic
- 1 & 1/2 tbsp. of sugar, brown
- 1 cup of ketchup, reduced sodium
- 3 tbsp. of butter, unsalted
- 1/4 cup of water, filtered
- 1/2 tsp. of celery salt
- 1 more tbsp. of flavoring, liquid smoke
- 2 tbsp. of Worcestershire sauce, reduced sodium
- 1 & 1/2 tsp. of mustard powder
- Kosher salt & ground pepper, as desired

Instructions:

1. Pour 2 tbsp. of liquid smoke on brisket. Rub it with garlic salt & onion salt. Roll in aluminum foil. Place in refrigerator overnight.

2. Preheat the oven to 300F. Place the brisket in large sized roasting pan. Cover. Bake for five to six hours. Remove pan

from the oven. Allow to cool and then slice it. Place slices back in pan.

3. Combine water, butter, ketchup, brown sugar, liquid smoke, celery salt, mustard and Worcestershire sauce in medium pan. Season as desired. Stir. Cook till boiling.

4. Pour the sauce over panned meat slices. Cover. Bake for an hour longer. Serve.

15 – Texas Onion Pie

This pie, made with sweet onions, is a great side for steak and potatoes. It tastes a lot like an onion au gratin, including cheese, eggs, flour and butter in a pie shell.

Makes 6 Servings

Cooking + Prep Time: 1 hour & 20 minutes

Ingredients:

- 6 chopped, large onions, sweet
- 1/2 cup of flour, all-purpose

- 1 prepared pie crust
- 2 eggs, large
- 1 stick of butter, unsalted
- 1 cup of cheese, Gruyere or Parmesan
- Kosher salt & ground pepper, as desired
- 2 tbsp. of chopped chives, fresh

Instructions:

1. Heat oven to 350F.

2. Melt butter in skillet over low heat. Add onions. Sauté till slightly browned and translucent.

3. Remove onions from heat. Pour in mixing bowl and allow to completely cool.

4. Place pie crust in oven. Brown and pre-heat.

5. In separate bowl, whisk eggs. Add and stir 3/4 cup cheese, plus the flour. Season as desired. Pour over cooled onions and stir.

6. Pour new mixture into warmed pie crust. Bake for 1/2 hour at 350F. Remove from oven. Add remainder of cheese over top. Place back in oven for 10 to 15 more minutes.

7. Remove pie from oven. Allow to cool a few minutes. Sprinkle chives over the top and serve.

16 – Texas Turkey Soup

This soup is so tasty, you'll love it for dinner or supper (remember Texans often call their midday meal dinner). In addition, it gives you another way to use leftover turkey from holiday parties.

Makes 6 Servings

Cooking + Prep Time: 55 minutes

Ingredients:

- 1 tbsp. of oil, olive
- 1/2 cup of onion, minced
- 3 minced garlic cloves
- 2 tsp. of chili powder
- 1/2 tsp. of cumin, ground
- 1/2 tsp. of oregano
- 4 cups of water, filtered
- 1 x 10 & 3/4-oz. can of tomato soup
- 1 x 28-oz. can of tomatoes, diced
- 1 cup of salsa
- 4 cups of cooked turkey, shredded
- 1 tbsp. of parsley, dried
- 3 bouillon cubes, chicken
- 1 x 14-oz can of rinsed, drained black beans
- 2 cups of corn, frozen
- 1/2 cup of sour cream, reduced fat
- 1/4 cup of cilantro, chopped

For topping:

- 6 cups of tortilla chips, corn
- 3/4 cup of green onions, chopped

- 1 cup of Monterey-Jack & cheddar cheese shreds
- 1/2 cup of cilantro, chopped
- Another 1/2 cup of sour cream, reduced fat

Instructions:

1. Heat oil in large sized sauce pan on med. heat. Add onions. Cook till they start softening.

2. Add the oregano, cumin, chili powder and garlic. Stir while cooking for a minute.

3. Add and stir tomato soup, water, salsa, tomatoes, parsley, bouillon and turkey. Bring to boil. Reduce heat. Allow to simmer for five minutes, till cubes of bouillon are dissolved.

4. Add the corn, black beans, cilantro and sour cream. Simmer for 25-30 minutes.

5. Add crushed tortilla chips, onions, cheese shreds, extra sour cream and cilantro. Serve.

17 – Chicken Casserole a la King Ranch

This is sometimes referred to as the State Dish of Texas, although other dishes cause people to make the same claim. This casserole dish includes tasty layers of creamy chicken, peppers, onions, tortillas, spices and cheese. Yum!

Makes 8 Servings

Cooking + Prep Time: 1 & 1/2 hour

Ingredients:

- 1 diced medium onion, white
- 1 diced bell pepper, orange
- 1 diced large bell pepper, green
- 3 tbsp. of oil, vegetable
- 2 cups of chopped, cooked chicken
- 1 can of chicken soup
- 1 can of mushroom soup
- 1 x 10-oz. can of diced tomatoes & green chilies
- 2 tsp. of cumin, ground
- 1 tsp. of chili powder
- 1/4 tsp. of salt, kosher
- 1/4 tsp. of garlic power
- 1/4 tsp. of pepper, ground
- 12 x 6" tortillas, corn
- 1 cup of cheese, cheddar
- 1 cup of cheese, Monterey Jack

Instructions:

1. Preheat the oven to 350F.

2. Heat the oil in large sized skillet on med-high. Sauté bell peppers and onions for five minutes, till tender.

3. Add and stir chicken soup, chicken, mushroom soup, tomatoes, chilies, chili powder, garlic powder, cumin, kosher salt & ground pepper. Sauté for five minutes.

4. Grease 13" x 9" casserole dish. Tear up corn tortillas. Line 1/3 of tortillas on bottom of casserole dish.

5. Spoon 1/3 chicken mixture over tortillas. Top that with 1/3 of cheese. Repeat these layers two more times.

6. Bake the casserole in 350F oven till it bubbles, 40 minutes or so. Raise oven temperature up to broil. Broil casserole till the top has turned a light golden brown, or two to three minutes. Remove from oven and allow to rest for about 10 minutes. Serve.

18 – Texas Style Pulled Pork

This pork is a Texas-style slow cooked meal. It's served on a toasted, buttered roll, and it is a favorite in many Texas households.

Makes 8 Servings

Cooking + Prep Time: 20 minutes + 5 hours slow cooker time

Ingredients:

- 1 tsp. of oil, vegetable
- 1 x 4-lb. roast, pork shoulder
- 1 cup of BBQ sauce, your preferred brand
- 1/2 cup of vinegar, apple cider
- 1/2 cup of chicken broth
- 1/4 cup of sugar, light brown
- 1 tbsp. of yellow mustard, store-bought
- 1 tbsp. of Worcestershire sauce, low sodium
- 1 tbsp. of chili powder
- 1 chopped onion, extra large
- 2 crushed cloves of garlic
- 1 & 1/2 tsp. of thyme, dried
- 8 split hamburger buns
- Butter – about 2 tbsp. + more if you need it

Instructions:

1. Pour oil in bottom of your slow cooker. Place pork roast in, as well. Add BBQ sauce, broth and vinegar.

2. Add and stir Worcestershire sauce, yellow mustard, brown sugar, garlic, onion, thyme and chili powder. Cover. Set at

High setting and cook for five to six hours, till you can easily use a fork to shred the roast.

3. Remove roast from slow cooker. Shred meat and return it to slow cooker. Stir into juices.

4. Spread insides of buns using butter. Toast them with the butter side facing down in skillet on med. heat. Spoon the pork onto buns and serve.

19 – Texas BBQ Chicken

There are few places to find better BBQ chicken than in the state of Texas. It is served at potlucks, picnics and family gatherings, and it's certainly a favorite.

Makes 12 servings

Cooking + Prep Time: 50 minutes

Ingredients:

- 2 fryer/broiler chickens – cut each into eight pieces
- Kosher salt
- Pepper, ground

- For BBQ sauce
- 2 tbsp. of oil, canola
- 2 chopped onions, small
- 2 cups of ketchup, low sodium
- 1/4 cup of lemon juice, fresh
- 2 tbsp. of sugar, brown
- 2 tbsp. of water, filtered
- 1/2 tsp. of garlic powder
- 1 tsp. of mustard, ground
- 1/4 tsp. of pepper, ground
- 1/8 tsp. of salt, kosher
- 1/8 tsp. of pepper sauce, hot

Instructions:

1. Sprinkle the pieces of chicken using kosher salt & ground pepper. Place on grill with the skin sides facing down. Leave them uncovered on rack on med. heat for 18-20 minutes.

2. To prepare sauce, heat oil on med. Add the onions and sauté till they are tender. Add in the rest of the sauce ingredients. Bring to boil. Lower heat. Leave uncovered and simmer for 8-10 minutes.

3. Turn the chicken and brush the pieces with BBQ sauce. Grill for 15 to 25 more minutes and brush often with the sauce, till internal thermometer reads 165F in breast area. Serve.

20 – Texas Shrimp Cocktail

Unlike many other shrimp cocktails, those made in Texas include serrano chilies and cilantro. This gives them a more authentic flavor, and it'll perk up your taste buds for sure.

Makes 8 Servings

Cooking + Prep Time: 25 minutes

Ingredients:

- 1 lb. of medium shrimp, cooked and chilled
- 1/2 cubed cucumber, large
- 1/2 cubed tomato, large
- 8 sliced green onions
- 1 oz. of chopped cilantro, fresh
- 1 sliced serrano pepper
- 1 x 8-oz. can of tomato sauce, low sodium
- 2 tbsp. of vinegar, white
- 1 lime, fresh

Instructions:

1. Combine the shrimp, tomatoes, cucumbers, cilantro, serrano pepper and green onions in large sized bowl. Add in vinegar and tomato sauce. Squeeze over the top with the lime juice. Serve.

21 – Chicken-Fried Steak

Grandmothers in Texas will happily share their secret recipe for chicken fried-steak. The meat is dredged in a mixture with flour and paprika, then dipped in beer, then re-dredged. It's fried in a pan, as you would imagine.

Makes 4 Servings

Cooking + Prep Time: 55 minutes

Ingredients:

- 4 x 1/2-lb. round steaks
- 2 cups of flour, all-purpose
- 2 tsp. of salt, kosher
- 2 tsp. of black pepper, ground
- 4 tbsp. of paprika, hot
- 1/4 tsp. of pepper, cayenne
- 2 eggs, large
- 1/2 cup of buttermilk, low-fat
- 1/2 cup of beer, your choice of brands
- 1/2 cup of oil, canola

Instructions:

1. Pound out meat till even, to tenderize it.

2. Mix the flour with paprika, cayenne pepper, 1 tsp. of kosher salt & 1 tsp. of ground pepper in medium-sized bowl. Set the bowl aside.

3. In separate bowl, whisk beer, buttermilk, eggs, 1 tsp. kosher salt & 1 tsp. ground pepper. Set that bowl aside, too.

4. Heat the oil in heavy, deep skillet

5. As oil heats, prepare steaks. Dredge them in flour mixture first and coat evenly. Then shake off excess flour.

6. Dip steaks in beer batter, then dip in flour again. Place steaks on plate.

7. Slide the steaks gently into the oil, one at a time, not overcrowding pan. Cook steaks for about three minutes each. Turn and cook for three additional minutes, till they are browned nicely.

8. Drain cooked steaks on plate lined with paper towels. Serve with Texas toast or mashed potatoes.

22 – Heart of Texas Beef & Bean Salad

This is one salad that could truthfully be called a meal by itself. It offers lettuce, pinto beans, tomatoes and ground beef and **Makes** a quite filling main dish – or you can make smaller servings and use as more of a side salad.

Makes 6 Servings

Cooking + Prep Time: 1/2 hour

Ingredients:

- 1 lb. of ground beef, lean
- 2 tbsp. of chili powder
- 1/2 tsp. of cumin, ground
- Kosher salt & ground pepper, as desired
- 1 shredded head of lettuce, iceberg
- 1 x 15 & 1/2 oz. can of pinto beans
- 1 cup of cheddar cheese shreds
- 2 cubed tomatoes
- 1/4 cup of cilantro, chopped
- 1 x 12-oz. pkg. of broken tortilla chips, corn

Optional:

- 1 de-seeded, chopped jalapeño pepper
- 1/2 cup of green onions, chopped
- 1 cup of salsa, mild or hot, as desired

Instructions:

1. Brown ground beef in large sized skillet on med-high. Sprinkle with the cumin and chili powder. Season as desired. When beef has cooked fully through, remove it from heat.

2. In large sized salad bowl, toss lettuce, cheese, tomatoes, pinto beans and cilantro together. Add ground beef & corn chips. Toss in salsa, jalapeños and green onions, as desired, and serve.

23 – Texas Cornbread

Ordinary cornbread, step aside. Texas cornbread is made with corn, cheddar cheese and jalapeño peppers. It's cooked in a heavy skillet, and it's just so "Texas" in its taste.

Makes 10 Servings

Cooking + Prep Time: 1 & 1/2 hour

Ingredients:

- 1 & 1/2 sticks of butter, unsalted
- 1 cup + 2 tbsp. of corn meal, stone ground

- 1 cup of flour, all-purpose, unbleached

- 1 tbsp. of salt, kosher

- 1 tbsp. of baking powder

- 1 cup of buttermilk or milk

- 2 tbsp. of brown sugar, packed

- 2 eggs, large

- 1/4 cup of fresh or frozen corn kernels

- 1-2 minced jalapeños – de-seed if you don't want the dish too hot

- 2 diced green onions, white part only

- 1 cup of grated cheddar cheese

- 1 tbsp. of oil, olive

Instructions:

1. Preheat oven to 375F. On stove top, melt butter on med. heat in 11" or 12" oven-safe, heavy skillet. Swirl the pan while cooking, coating bottom and sides with butter till butter has turned deep brown in color and is no longer foaming. Don't let the butter burn.

2. Pour butter in small sized bowl. Allow it to cool a bit. Don't wipe out skillet.

3. Mix 1 cup corn meal with salt, flour and baking soda together in medium sized bowl.

4. In small bowl holding your cooled butter, add and whisk in butter milk, eggs and brown sugar. Add liquid mixture to flour mixture. Stir till barely blended. Add and stir corn, jalapeños, cheese and green onions.

5. Heat skillet back up if needed. Pour batter in it. Put skillet in oven. Bake till top has turned golden brown in color and edges start pulling away from pan sides. This usually takes between 30 and 40 minutes or so.

6. Allow mixture to cool in skillet for 8-10 minutes. Slice and serve warm.

24 – Texas Style Jambalaya

From the Creole influence in the Southern US comes Texas Jambalaya. It's a filling and hearty meal and you'll only have to clean up one pot when you're done preparing it.

Makes 6 Servings

Cooking + Prep Time: 50 minutes

Ingredients:

- 2 tbsp. of oil, olive
- 1 cup of onions, diced
- 1/2 cup of diced bell pepper, green

- 1/2 cup of celery, diced
- 1 & 1/2 tsp. of garlic, chopped
- 1 cup of white rice, long-grain, converted
- 4 oz. of sliced sausage, smoked
- 4 oz. of cubed ham, cooked
- 2 x 10-oz. cans of diced tomatoes & green chilies
- 1 cup of broth, chicken
- 1/4 tsp. of thyme, dried
- 1 bay leaf
- 2 x 15-oz. cans of undrained beans, ranch-style

Instructions:

1. Heat the oil in large sized pan on med. heat. Sauté the celery, onion and green pepper till onions have become translucent and soft. Add and stir garlic. Cook for a minute longer.

2. Add the sausage, ham and rice. Cook for two to three minutes. Coat rice with the oil and stir frequently.

3. Pour in the tomatoes and broth. Add bay leaf and thyme. Bring up to boil. Reduce the heat. Cover pan. Simmer for 20-25 minutes till liquid has been absorbed. Add and stir beans. Mix thoroughly and heat fully through. Serve.

25 – Green Rice - Arroz Verde

This is Tex-Mex cooking at its best. It's made with fresh vegetables sautéed and then cooked into rice. It's usually served with refried or pinto beans as side dishes.

Makes 6 Servings

Cooking + Prep Time: 1 hour & 10 minutes

Ingredients:

- 6 green onions with diced white bulbs & chopped green parts set aside.
- 2 diced cloves of garlic

- 2 chopped bell peppers, green
- 3/4 cup of flaked parsley
- 3 cups of white rice, uncooked
- 9 bouillon cubes, chicken
- 1/2 lime, fresh
- 6 cups of water, filtered

Instructions:

1. Sauté bell peppers, green onions, bouillon cubes and parsley, till bell peppers soften a little, usually 10 minutes or so. Add garlic. Sauté for a minute longer.

2. Add six cups of filtered water and add rice. Season as desired. Place lid on the pot. Turn the heat to low. Cooking time from here to finish is between 30 and 45 minutes.

3. Add 1/2 lime juice. Sprinkle with tops from green onions. Serve.

The desserts are somehow tastier in Texas than they seem to be everywhere else... Here are some of the best...

26 – Stockman's Buttermilk Pie

These silky, stupendous pies are served all through the year, generally with sweet iced tea. Some cooks add a bit of nutmeg, just for a bit of a different taste.

Makes 6-8 Servings

Cooking + Prep Time: 1 hour & 25 minutes

Ingredients:

- 9 eggs, large
- 3 sticks of melted margarine
- 3 tsp. of vanilla, pure
- 1 dash salt, kosher
- 4 & 1/2 cups of sugar, granulated
- 9 tbsp. of flour, all-purpose
- 1 & 1/2 cups of butter milk, reduced fat
- 3/4 tsp. of nutmeg
- 2 pie crusts, unbaked

Instructions:

1. Preheat the oven to 425F. Lightly beat the eggs. Blend all remaining ingredients.

2. Pour the mixture into the pie crusts and bake the pies for 8-10 minutes.

3. Lower oven heat to 350F. Cook pies till firm. This typically takes an hour or so. Serve.

27 – Texas Red Velvet Cake

This is a cake with beautiful texture and a mildly chocolate flavor. Its claim to fame in Texas, and elsewhere, is its stunning red color. It is typically covered with white, thick frosting, which sets the redness of the cake apart even more.

Makes 10 Servings

Cooking + Prep Time: 1 hour & 20 minutes

Ingredients:

- 2 & 1/4 cups of sifted flour, all-purpose
- 1 tsp. of salt, kosher

- 2 tbsp. of cocoa powder
- 1/2 cup shortening, vegetable
- 2 x 1-oz. bottles food coloring, red
- 1 & 1/2 cups of sugar, granulated
- 2 eggs, large
- 1 cup of butter milk, reduced fat
- 1 tsp. of vanilla extract, pure
- 1 tsp. of vinegar, white
- 1 tsp. of baking soda

Instructions:

1. Preheat the oven to 350F. Grease & flour 2 x 9" cake pans.

2. Combine sifted flour with salt. Set bowl aside.

3. Place cocoa in small sized glass bowl. Gradually add food coloring and stir till mixture has a smooth texture. Set bowl aside.

4. Cream shortening & granulated sugar together. Beat for four to five minutes, using medium speed on electric mixer, till you have a fluffy mixture.

5. Add eggs, one after another, and beat for 35 seconds or so after every addition.

6. Set mixer to low speed. Add flour mixture to granulated sugar mixture, alternating with vanilla and butter milk. Scrape sides down as needed.

7. Add the cocoa mixture and mix till your batter has a uniform color. Don't beat too long.

8. Mix baking soda and vinegar in small sized bowl. Expect the mixture to foam. Briefly stir and mix them together. Add to your cake batter and incorporate thoroughly, without beating it.

9. Pour batter into cake pans. Bake at 350F for 25-30 minutes, till cake tester will come back clean. Place layers of cake on rack for 8-10 minutes to cool. Assemble layers and frost. Allow the full cake to cool completely before serving.

28 – Mesquite Cookies

These chocolate chip cookies are kissed with mesquite's hearty, smoky taste. It is definitely a favorite cookie in the Lone Star State.

Makes 12-16 cookies

Cooking + Prep Time: 50 minutes

Ingredients:

- 1 stick of softened butter, unsalted
- 3/4 cup of sugar, brown
- 1 tsp. of vanilla, pure

- 1 egg, large
- 1/4 tsp. of salt, kosher
- 1 tsp. of baking soda
- 1/2 cup of flour, mesquite bean
- 1/2 cup of flour, wheat or white
- 1/2 cup of oats, rolled
- 1/2 cup of your favorites from these mix-in Ingredients:
- Raisins, nuts or chocolate chips

Instructions:

1. Cream the butter and granulated sugar. Add and stir egg and vanilla till barely incorporated.

2. Stir the baking soda, salt and flour together in separate bowl. Combine this with the wet mixture. Add rolled oats plus any mix-ins you selected.

3. Scoop small sized dough balls on a cookie sheet. Bake for 10-15 minutes at 350F till browned lightly. Serve.

29 – Strawberry – Rhubarb Pie

When springtime arrives, you'll have fresh rhubarb to cook, and this pie is among the recipes that people long for, when they think of rhubarb. The strawberries add sweetness, and sugar is usually added, as well.

Makes 8 Servings

Cooking + Prep Time: 1 & 3/4 hour

Ingredients:

- 1 cup of sugar, granulated
- 1/2 cup of flour, all-purpose

- 1 lb. of chopped rhubarb, fresh
- 2 pints of strawberries, fresh
- 9" double pie crust
- 2 tbsp. of butter, unsalted
- 1 egg yolk from large egg
- 2 tbsp. of sugar, white

Instructions:

1. Preheat the oven to 400F.

2. Mix cup of sugar and flour in large sized bowl. Add rhubarb and strawberries. Toss with flour and sugar. Allow to stand for 1/2 hour.

3. Pour the filling in to the pie crust. Then dot the top of it with butter. Cover with the top pie crust and seal the edges of bottom and top crusts using water.

4. Apply egg yolk to the top of the pie with a pastry brush. Sprinkle top with sugar. Cut some small holes in the top to allow steam to escape.

5. Bake in 400F oven for 35-40 minutes, till brown and bubbly. Set on rack to cool. Serve.

30 – Peach Crisp

Without offending apple pie, Texans love their peach crisp. It's a true celebration of peaches, and it doesn't even take too long to whip the dessert up.

Makes 6 Servings

Cooking + Prep Time: 1 hour & 10 minutes

Ingredients:

- 6 cups of peeled, sliced peaches

- 1 tbsp. of lemon juice, fresh
- 1/4 cup of honey, organic
- 3/4 cup of flour, all-purpose
- 3/4 cup of oats, rolled
- 4 cups of brown sugar, packed finely
- 2 tbsp. of sugar, lavender
- 1/2 tsp. of cinnamon, ground
- 1/2 cup of butter, softened
- 6 scoops of ice cream, lavender

Instructions:

1. Place the peaches in 9x9" pan.

2. Sprinkle with fresh lemon juice. Drizzle with honey.

3. Mix remaining ingredients together with a fork in a medium sized bowl.

4. Sprinkle this mixture over the peaches evenly.

5. Bake at 350F for 30-40 minutes, till top has turned a golden brown color.

6. Serve while still warm and top with ice cream, if desired.

Conclusion

This Texas cookbook has shown you...

How to use different ingredients to affect unique Southwestern tastes in dishes both well-known and rare. Texas cuisine has shot to international acclaim of late.

How can you include Texas tastes in your home recipes?

You can...

- Make breakfasts from the Lone Star State, which you may not have known about. They are just as tasty as they look.
- Learn to cook with hot and mild salsas, which are widely used in Texas recipes. Find them in the sauce or ethnic section of food markets.
- Enjoy making the delectable Tex-Mex dishes of the Southwestern United States, including BBQ, tacos and Mexican favorites. These are mainstays in the region, and there are SO many ways to make them great.
- Make dishes using pinto and refried beans, which are often used in Texas cooking.

- Make various types of desserts like mesquite cookies and peach crisp, which will tempt your family's sweet tooth.

Have fun experimenting! Enjoy the results!